With love and bedtime kisses for Joseph Daniel, John Cody, Rebekah Louise, and Mary Catherine.

Copyright © 1996 by Educational Publishing Concepts, Inc., Wheaton, Illinois

Published by Concordia Publishing House
3558 S. Jefferson Avenue, St. Louis, MO 63118-3968
Manufactured in the United States of America

1 2 3 4 5 6 7 8 9 10   05 04 03 02 01 00 99 98 97 96

My First Bedtime Blessing Book

Mary Harwell Sayler

Illustrated by Christopher Gray

CPH
SAINT LOUIS

Outside the sun is resting.
It's time to go to bed.
I lay down on my pillow
And pull the covers around my head.

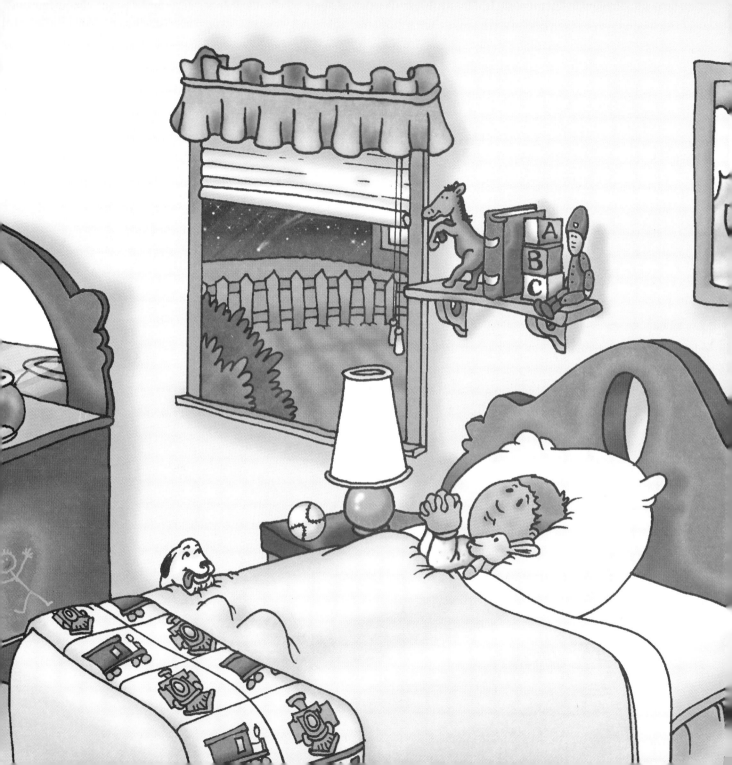

God bless the sun
That warmed the day.
God bless my friends
Who came to play.

God bless the stars
In the shining sky.
God bless the round-faced moon
Up high.

God bless the rain,
Softly falling down.
God bless the water,
Wind, and ground.

God bless the trees
And birds and squirrels.
God bless my town,
And the whole wide world!

God bless the grass
And flowers that bloom.
God bless my house
And every room.

God bless my church,
And the people there.
God bless the songs
And every prayer.

God bless each place
That I have been.
God bless my family,
And my friends.

God bless Daddy,
Mommy too.
God bless me,
And God bless you.

God bless my sleep
As off I nod.
God bless this night.
And God bless God!